From Side Hustle to CEO

Get ready to unlock your entrepreneurial potential and take your business to new heights

I0409284

JUDE UNIMNA

CONTENTS

INTRODUCTION

Congratulations on embarking on a journey to transform your side hustle into a thriving business! In this comprehensive book, we dive deep into the essential steps and strategies required to elevate your entrepreneurial potential and achieve long-term success.

Chapter 1 explores "The Power of Side Hustles: Exploring Entrepreneurial Potential," highlighting the unique advantages and opportunities that side hustles offer. Discover how your side hustle can become the foundation for building your dream business.

In Chapter 2, "Identifying Profitable Opportunities: Finding Your Niche," we guide you through the process of identifying a profitable and fulfilling niche for your business. Uncover the key factors that make a niche market attractive and learn how to position yourself for success.

Setting a strong foundation is crucial, and Chapter 3, "Laying the Foundation: Planning and Setting Goals," provides practical insights on effective planning, goal setting, and creating a roadmap for your entrepreneurial journey.

Your business's identity and brand are pivotal to its success, and Chapter 4, "Building a Strong Brand: Crafting Your Business Identity," delves into the strategies for creating a compelling brand that resonates with your target audience and sets you apart from competitors.

Effective marketing is essential for any business, and in Chapter 5, "Marketing Strategies for Side Hustlers: Reaching Your Target Audience," we explore various marketing tactics tailored to side hustlers. Learn how to reach and engage your target audience with limited resources.

Chapter 6, "The Art of Sales: Convincing and Closing Deals," equips you with the necessary sales skills and techniques to confidently navigate the sales process. Master the art of persuasion and negotiation to drive growth and increase revenue.

Scaling up your business is a significant milestone, and Chapter 7, "Scaling Up: Strategies for Sustainable Growth," provides insights into scalable strategies and frameworks that will help you expand your business while maintaining stability and profitability.

Financial management is a critical aspect of business success, and Chapter 8, "Managing Finances: Budgeting and Cash Flow for Success," offers practical guidance on budgeting, cash flow management, and maintaining a healthy financial foundation.

Transitioning from an entrepreneur to a CEO requires a shift in mindset and skills. Chapter 9, "Transitioning to CEO: Leadership Skills for Long-Term Success," focuses on the qualities and abilities you need to cultivate to lead your business to sustainable growth and prosperity.

By the end of this book you'll have gained invaluable insights and actionable strategies to elevate your side hustle, transform it into a successful business, and step into the role of a confident CEO. Get ready to unlock your entrepreneurial potential and take your business to new heights!

Chapter 1: The Power of Side Hustles: Exploring Entrepreneurial Potential

You can't have a million dollar dream with a minimum wage work ethics ~Stephen C.Hogan

Hustle until your haters ask if you are hiring ~Steve Maraboli

In today's dynamic and ever-changing business landscape, side hustles have emerged as a powerful avenue for individuals to explore their entrepreneurial potential. Gone are the days when a single career path defined our professional journey. The rise of the gig economy, advancements in technology, and changing work dynamics have opened up a world of opportunities for those willing to tap into their entrepreneurial spirit. To fully appreciate the power of side hustles, one must first embrace the side hustle mindset. It involves adopting an entrepreneurial mindset characterized by creativity, adaptability, and a willingness to take calculated risks. Side hustles provide the ideal environment for nurturing these traits, as they encourage individuals to step outside their comfort zones, explore new interests, and cultivate skills beyond their primary professions. This chapter delves into the transformative power of side hustles, highlighting the benefits and possibilities they offer to individuals seeking to carve their own paths in the business world.

Diversifying Income Streams:

One of the primary advantages of side hustles is the ability to diversify income streams. Relying solely on a single source of income can be risky in today's uncertain economic climate. Side hustles offer a buffer, allowing individuals to generate additional revenue streams and reduce their dependence on a single paycheck. This diversification not only provides financial stability but also creates opportunities for wealth creation and long-term financial independence.

Discovering Passion and Purpose:

Side hustles provide a platform for individuals to pursue their passions and uncover their true purpose. Often, traditional careers may not allow for the exploration of personal interests or the pursuit of meaningful work. Engaging in a side hustle allows individuals to discover what truly ignites their passion and aligns with their values. Whether it's turning a hobby into a business or addressing a societal need, side hustles offer the freedom to explore and contribute in ways that bring fulfillment and purpose to one's life.

Flexibility and Work-Life Balance:

The flexibility offered by side hustles is a significant draw for many aspiring entrepreneurs. Unlike traditional 9-to-5 jobs, side hustles can be tailored to fit around existing commitments and responsibilities. This flexibility enables individuals to pursue their entrepreneurial endeavors while maintaining a healthy work-life balance. Side hustles allow for greater control over one's time, making it possible to juggle multiple roles and responsibilities without feeling overwhelmed.

Testing the Waters:

Starting a full-fledged business can be intimidating and involve considerable risk. Side hustles offer a low-risk environment for testing business ideas, validating market demand, and refining entrepreneurial skills. By starting small and gradually scaling up, individuals can assess the viability of their ventures, learn from their experiences, and make informed decisions about their future entrepreneurial pursuits.

Creating Networks and Opportunities:

Engaging in a side hustle expands an individual's network and opens doors to new opportunities. Collaborating with like-minded individuals, connecting with potential customers, and leveraging online platforms can all contribute to the growth and success of a side hustle. Networking within entrepreneurial communities and attending industry events provides valuable insights, mentorship, and potential partnerships that can accelerate the journey from side hustle to a thriving business.

Conclusion

The power of side hustles lies in their ability to unleash untapped potential, foster entrepreneurial skills, and open up a world of possibilities. Embracing a side hustle mindset, diversifying income streams, pursuing passion, enjoying flexibility, testing ideas, and expanding networks are just some of the ways side hustles empower individuals to explore their entrepreneurial potential. By embarking on this entrepreneurial journey, individuals can uncover hidden talents, create meaningful impact, and ultimately forge their own paths to success. Remember, the journey from a side hustle to a successful business begins with embracing the power of side hustles and recognizing the endless opportunities they offer. As you embark on this transformative journey, keep an open mind, embrace the entrepreneurial mindset, and let your side hustle become the catalyst for realizing your full potential in the world of business.

Chapter 2: Identifying Profitable Opportunities: Finding Your Niche

I think the greatest people in society carved represented the unique expression of their combination of talents, and if everyone has the luxury of expressing the unique combination of talents in this world, our society would be transformed overnight ~Neil DeGrasse Tyson

Finding a profitable niche is not just a luxury; it's a necessity. In this chapter, we will delve deeper into the process of identifying profitable opportunities and guide you on how to find your niche effectively. By narrowing your focus, understanding your target market, and positioning yourself as an expert, you can not only survive but thrive in the competitive business world. Let's embark on the journey of discovering your niche and unlocking its full potential. To lay a strong foundation for your entrepreneurial journey, it is crucial to understand the significance of finding your niche. A niche allows you to concentrate your efforts, resources, and expertise on a specific market segment. It enables you to tailor your products or services to cater to the unique needs and desires of a particular group of customers. By specializing in a niche, you position yourself as a trusted authority, gain a competitive advantage, and create a strong brand presence. Let us take a look at how you can identify and create a profitable niche for your business

Analyzing Market Trends and Consumer Behavior

Before identifying a profitable niche, it's essential to conduct comprehensive market research and analyze current trends and consumer behavior. Stay up-to-date with industry reports, market studies, and relevant publications to gain insights into emerging opportunities. Pay attention to changing consumer preferences, technological advancements, and shifts in demographics. By understanding market dynamics, you can identify gaps and anticipate future needs within your target market.

Assessing Your Passion and Expertise

Finding a profitable niche requires a careful evaluation of your own passions, interests, and expertise. What subjects or industries excite you? What skills or knowledge do you possess that sets you apart? Identifying a niche that aligns with your personal interests not only ensures your own satisfaction but also helps you navigate challenges with enthusiasm and dedication. Capitalize on your strengths and unique experiences to establish credibility and differentiate yourself from competitors.

Defining Your Target Market

Once you have narrowed down potential niches, it is crucial to define your target market precisely. Understanding your ideal customers is the cornerstone of successful niche marketing. Consider their demographics, psychographics, motivations, and pain points. Develop detailed buyer personas that represent your target audience. This exercise will help you tailor your products, services, and marketing strategies to cater to their specific needs effectively.

Conducting Competitor Analysis

To carve out a profitable niche, it is essential to conduct a thorough analysis of your competitors. Identify both direct and indirect competitors in your chosen niche. Study their strengths, weaknesses, market positioning, and pricing strategies. Analyze their customer feedback, online presence, and marketing efforts. By gaining a comprehensive understanding of your competition, you can identify gaps and areas where you can offer unique value propositions.

Testing and Validating Your Niche

Before fully committing to a niche, it is vital to test and validate its profitability. Create a prototype, conduct surveys, or offer a limited trial of your product or service to gather feedback from potential customers. Engage with your target market and listen to their responses and suggestions. Iterate and refine your offering based on their input. Validating your niche through real-world feedback minimizes risks and increases your chances of success.

Refining Your Brand and Marketing Strategy

Once you have validated your niche, it's time to refine your brand and marketing strategy to establish a strong market presence. Craft a compelling brand story that resonates with your target audience. Develop key messages that highlight the unique benefits of your products or services. Tailor your marketing channels to reach your niche market effectively. Leverage social media, content marketing, search engine optimization, and targeted advertising to connect with your audience authentically.

Conclusion

Identifying a profitable niche is not a one-time event; it's an ongoing process that requires continuous monitoring, adaptation, and innovation. By understanding market trends, analyzing consumer behavior, leveraging your passions and expertise, defining your target market, conducting competitor analysis, and validating your niche, you can position yourself for long-term success. Embrace the challenges and opportunities that come with finding your niche and stay committed to delivering exceptional value to your target audience. With dedication, persistence, and the right strategies, your niche business can thrive and become a profitable venture.

Chapter 3: Laying the Foundation: Planning and Setting Goals

Without a plan, even the most brilliant business can get lost. You need to have goals, create milestones and have a strategy in place to set yourself up for success
~Yogi Berra

Setting goals and creating a comprehensive plan are crucial steps in achieving success in any aspect of life. Whether you're embarking on a personal journey, starting a business, or pursuing a career, laying a solid foundation through effective planning and goal-setting is essential. In This chapter, we will delve into the importance of planning and setting goals, explore various techniques and strategies, and provide practical advice to help you chart a path towards your desired outcomes.

Planning is the process of envisioning your future and outlining the steps required to reach your desired destination. It serves as a roadmap, providing direction, structure, and organization to your efforts. Without a well-thought-out plan, you risk wandering aimlessly and missing out on opportunities for growth and progress. Before embarking on any planning endeavor, it's crucial to have a clear vision of what you want to achieve. Take the time to reflect on your aspirations, values, and passions. Visualize your ideal future and set your sights on that vision. A compelling and inspiring vision will serve as the driving force behind your goals and planning efforts. Setting goals is a fundamental aspect of effective planning. A widely recognized framework for goal-setting is the SMART acronym, which stands for Specific, Measurable, Achievable, Relevant, and Time-bound.

- Specific: Clearly define your goals in specific terms. Instead of saying, "I want to start a business," specify the type of business, the industry, and the target audience.

- Measurable: Establish metrics or indicators to track your progress. This allows you to measure your success and make adjustments along the way.

- Achievable: Set goals that are challenging yet attainable. Consider your resources, skills, and limitations, ensuring that your goals are within your reach.

- Relevant: Align your goals with your overall vision and purpose. Make sure they are meaningful and relevant to your long-term aspirations.

- Time-bound: Set deadlines and establish a timeline for achieving your goals. This adds a sense of urgency and helps you stay focused and motivated.

Once you have identified your goals, break them down into smaller, manageable tasks. Breaking goals into bite-sized pieces not only makes them less overwhelming but also provides a clear roadmap for action. Create a step-by-step plan outlining the specific actions required to accomplish each goal. This process enhances clarity and enables you to make progress incrementally.

One thing you must know is that every plan encounters obstacles and unforeseen circumstances. It is essential to anticipate potential challenges and risks and develop contingency plans to mitigate them. Identify the possible roadblocks that may hinder your progress and brainstorm strategies to overcome them. This proactive approach ensures that you are prepared to handle setbacks and maintain your momentum. While planning is crucial, it is equally important to remain flexible and adaptable. Recognize that circumstances may change, and adjustments to your plan may be necessary. Embrace the concept of agile planning, allowing for modifications and refinements along the way. This flexibility enables you to respond effectively to changing conditions and seize new opportunities.

Conclusion

Planning and setting goals lay the foundation for success, providing a roadmap to guide your actions and decisions. By defining your vision, setting SMART goals, breaking them down into manageable tasks, anticipating challenges, and remaining flexible, you empower yourself to navigate the complexities of life and achieve your desired outcomes. Remember, the process of planning is not set in stone; it is a dynamic and iterative process. Embrace it, stay committed, and watch your dreams transform into reality.

Chapter 4: Building a Strong Brand: Crafting Your Business Identity

A product can be quickly outdated, but a successful brand s timeless ~Stephen King

A business brand refers to the unique identity and images that your company will create to differentiate itself from its competitors in the market. It encompasses various elements such as your company's name, logo, design, messaging, values and overall perception by customers. A strong business brand helps to establish trust, recognition and loyalty among consumers, allowing your company to stand out and make a lasting impression in the marketplace. Building a strong brand is essential for your business growth. This chapter will guide you through the process of crafting a powerful business identity that resonates with your target audience, establishes trust, and sets you apart from the competition. So let us delve straight to how you can define your brand identity and stand out.

Understanding Your Target Audience

To build a strong brand, you must have a deep understanding of your target audience. Conduct thorough market research to identify their needs, preferences, and aspirations. This information will help you tailor your brand identity to resonate with your target customers.

Establishing Brand Values

Determine the core values that will define your brand. These values should align with your business objectives and reflect what your brand stands for. By clearly defining your brand values, you will create a foundation for building a consistent and authentic brand identity.

Crafting Your Brand Personality

Just like individuals, brands can have personalities. Think about the traits and characteristics that you want your brand to convey. Are you aiming for a friendly, approachable tone or a more professional and authoritative voice? Define your brand's personality to ensure consistent messaging across all touchpoints

Now let us take a look on how you can develop Visual Brand Elements

Creating a Memorable Logo

Your logo is the visual centerpiece of your brand identity. It should be unique, visually appealing, and easily recognizable. Work with professional designers to create a logo that embodies your brand's values and resonates with your target audience.

Selecting Brand Colors

Colors evoke emotions and play a crucial role in brand recognition. Choose a color palette that aligns with your brand personality and creates the desired emotional response. Ensure consistency in using these colors across all marketing materials and platforms.

Choosing Typography

Typography contributes to your brand's visual identity. Select fonts that complement your brand personality and are legible across various mediums. A consistent typography style will help reinforce your brand's recognition and professionalism.

The following points will help you understand how to draft brand message

Developing a Brand Voice

Your brand voice is the tone and style of communication used in your messaging. It should align with your brand personality and resonate with your target audience. Whether it's conversational, authoritative, or playful, maintain consistency in your brand voice across all marketing channels.

Creating a Compelling Tagline

Craft a concise and memorable tagline that captures the essence of your brand. It should be unique, succinct, and communicate the value proposition or key benefits of your business. A well-crafted tagline can leave a lasting impression on your audience.

Writing Brand Stories

Humans connect with stories, so use storytelling techniques to communicate your brand's values and mission. Share compelling narratives that showcase how your brand solves problems or creates positive change. Authentic and relatable brand stories help build emotional connections with your audience. Once you have successfully built your brand the next thing to think of is how to manage your brand well and be consistent. The following steps will guide you

Maintaining Brand Consistency

Consistency is key to building a strong brand. Ensure that all visual and verbal brand elements remain consistent across different platforms and marketing channels. This consistency builds recognition and fosters trust with your audience.

Training and Empowering Employees

Your employees are ambassadors of your brand. Train them to understand your brand values, messaging, and tone of voice. Empower them to embody the brand's identity in their interactions with customers, as they can significantly influence brand perception.

Monitoring and Evolving Your Brand

Monitor how your brand is perceived in the market through customer feedback, social media, and market research. Stay adaptable and open to evolving your brand strategy as your business grows and consumer preferences change. Regularly evaluate your brand identity to ensure it remains relevant and resonates with your target audience.

Conclusion

Crafting a strong brand identity is a continuous process that requires careful thought and execution. By defining your brand's values, developing visual brand elements, crafting compelling messaging, and maintaining consistency, you can establish a brand that stands out, builds trust, and connects deeply with your target audience. Building a strong brand takes time and effort, but the rewards are worth it, as a well-crafted brand identity can be a powerful asset for your business's long-term success.

Chapter 5: Marketing Strategies for Side Hustlers

strategy is figuring out what not to do ~Steve Jobs

In today's gig economy, side hustles have become increasingly popular as a way to generate additional income or pursue a passion project. However, for side hustlers to succeed, effective marketing strategies are crucial. Marketing strategies are planned and coordinated efforts that companies undertake to promote their products or services, reach their target audience, and achieve business goals. These strategies involve understanding the market and customers, setting clear objectives, and developing specific tactics. Promotional activities like advertising, PR, and social media are utilized to engage the target audience. Regular monitoring and analysis help measure effectiveness and make data-driven decisions for optimization. Marketing strategies aim to reach customers, build loyalty, and drive business growth. This chapter will delve into various marketing tactics that side hustlers can employ to promote their ventures, reach their target audience, and ultimately achieve their business goals.

Understanding Your Target Audience

Before diving into marketing tactics, it's essential to have a clear understanding of your target audience. By identifying your ideal customers, you can tailor your marketing efforts to resonate with them effectively. Consider factors such as demographics, psychographics, interests, and pain points. Conducting market research, surveys, or even analyzing data from similar businesses can provide valuable insights.

Crafting a Compelling Value Proposition

With a deep understanding of your target audience, you can now develop a compelling value proposition for your side hustle. Your value proposition should clearly communicate the unique benefits and value that your product or service offers to customers. It should address how your side hustle solves a problem or fulfills a need better than competitors. A strong value proposition forms the foundation of your marketing strategy.

Building a Strong Online Presence

In today's digital age, having a strong online presence is critical for any business, including side hustles. Here are some key elements to consider:

1. Professional Website: Create a well-designed, user-friendly website that showcases your side hustle. Include information about your products or services, pricing, contact details, and compelling content that resonates with your target audience.

 2. Social Media Platforms: Determine which social media platforms your target audience frequents the most and establish a presence there. Engage with your audience, share valuable content, run promotions, and respond to comments and messages promptly.

3. Content Marketing: Develop a content marketing strategy to provide value to your audience and establish yourself as an expert in your niche. Create blog posts, videos, podcasts, or infographics that address your audience's pain points and share them on your website and social media platforms.

4. Search Engine Optimization (SEO): Optimize your website and content for search engines to improve your visibility in organic search results. Research relevant keywords, create high-quality content, and ensure your website is technically optimized for search engines.

Utilizing Email Marketing

Email marketing remains one of the most effective marketing channels for side hustlers. Building an email list allows you to directly communicate with your audience, nurture leads, and drive conversions. Consider the following strategies:

1. Lead Magnet: Offer a valuable free resource, such as an ebook, checklist, or mini-course, in exchange for visitors' email addresses. This helps grow your email list and establish your authority in your niche.

2. Newsletter: Send regular newsletters to your subscribers, providing updates, exclusive offers, and valuable content. Personalize your emails and segment your list based on subscribers' preferences to increase engagement and conversions.

3. Automated Email Sequences: Set up automated email sequences to welcome new subscribers, nurture leads, and encourage them to take specific actions, such as making a purchase or signing up for a service.

Harnessing the Power of Influencer Marketing

Collaborating with influencers in your niche can significantly boost your side hustle's visibility and credibility. Consider the following approaches to influencer marketing:

1. Research and Outreach: Identify influencers whose values align with your brand and have an engaged audience. Reach out to them with a personalized pitch, offering collaboration opportunities such as product reviews, sponsored content, or giveaways.

2. Affiliate Marketing: Set up an affiliate program where influencers earn a commission for every sale they generate. This incentivizes them to promote your products or services actively.

3. Guest Collaborations: Collaborate with influencers on joint projects, such as webinars, podcasts, or co-created content. This helps you tap into their audience and gain exposure to new potential customers.

Measuring and Analyzing Results

To ensure the effectiveness of your marketing efforts, it's crucial to measure and analyze your results. Utilize analytics tools to track key metrics such as website traffic, conversion rates, email open rates, and social media engagement. Regularly review the data to identify what's working well and areas that require improvement. This data-driven approach allows you to refine your marketing strategies over time.

Conclusion

Marketing strategies play a vital role in the success of any side hustle. By understanding your target audience, crafting a compelling value proposition, establishing a strong online presence, utilizing email marketing, harnessing the power of influencer marketing, and measuring your results, you can effectively promote your side hustle and achieve your business goals. Embrace experimentation, adapt to changes in your industry, and continuously refine your marketing tactics to stay ahead of the competition and maximize your side hustle's potential for success.

Chapter 6: Mastering the Art of Convincing and Closing Deals

Expect the yes. Embrace the no. that's how you master the close!

This chapter aims to equip you with practical tips and a friendly approach to help you become a persuasive negotiator and successful deal closer. Whether you are a seasoned sales professional or just starting your entrepreneurial journey, the strategies and techniques shared here will empower you to build strong relationships, win over clients, and seal the deal with confidence. So, let's dive in!

Building Genuine Connections

When it comes to convincing and closing deals, building genuine connections with your potential clients is essential. People do business with people they know, like, and trust. Take the time to understand your clients' needs, preferences, and challenges. Show genuine interest by actively listening and asking insightful questions. By empathizing with their situation, you can establish a strong rapport and foster a sense of trust, making it easier to convince them of the value your product or service offers.

Storytelling and Emotional Appeal

Stories have an incredible power to captivate and engage people. Incorporate storytelling techniques into your sales pitch to create a compelling narrative around your product or service. Highlight how it has positively impacted others, using real-life examples and success stories. Appeal to the emotions of your potential clients by painting a vivid picture of how your solution can transform their lives or businesses. By tapping into their aspirations and desires, you can effectively convince them of the benefits they will experience.

Tailoring Your Message

One size does not fit all when it comes to convincing and closing deals. Every client is unique, with their own set of needs and preferences. Customize your message and approach to align with their specific requirements. Show that you have done your homework by researching their industry, competitors, and pain points. Use this knowledge to demonstrate how your offering is the perfect fit for their particular situation. When clients feel that you understand their specific challenges, they are more likely to trust your solution and move closer to a deal.

Demonstrating Value

To convince potential clients, it's essential to clearly articulate the value your product or service brings to the table. Focus on the tangible benefits they will gain by choosing your solution. Explain how it solves their problems, saves them time or money, or enhances their productivity. Provide concrete examples and data to back up your claims. Visual aids such as charts, infographics, or demos can also be powerful tools to showcase the value and impact of your offering.

Handling Objections

Objections are a natural part of the sales process. Instead of avoiding or dismissing them, see objections as an opportunity to address concerns and build trust. Listen attentively to your clients' objections and respond in a thoughtful and respectful manner. Take the time to understand their underlying reasons for hesitating. Then, provide clear and persuasive counterarguments, emphasizing the unique advantages and benefits your product or service offers. By addressing objections head-on, you demonstrate your expertise and commitment to finding the best solution for your clients.

Creating Win-Win Solutions

Closing deals successfully requires a win-win mindset. Your goal should be to create a partnership where both parties benefit and feel satisfied with the agreement. Look for opportunities to align your interests with those of your clients. Seek to understand their long-term goals and explore how your solution can help them achieve those goals. Be open to negotiation and flexible in finding creative solutions that meet both parties' needs. A win-win approach not only strengthens the business relationship but also lays the foundation for future collaboration and mutual success.

The Art of Closing

Closing the deal is the culmination of all your efforts. When the time is right, confidently ask for the close. Summarize the key points of your discussion, highlighting the benefits and value your solution brings. Address any remaining concerns or questions and provide reassurance. Clearly communicate the next steps and timelines to solidify the agreement. Remember to maintain a friendly and approachable demeanor throughout the closing process, making your potential clients feel comfortable and confident in their decision to work with you.

Conclusion

Remember that building genuine connections, using storytelling techniques, tailoring your message, demonstrating value, handling objections, creating win-win solutions, and mastering the art of closing are all essential elements of the deal-closing process. Continuously practice and refine your skills, adapting them to different situations and clients. With dedication and a friendly approach, you will become a persuasive negotiator and achieve remarkable success in closing deals.

Chapter 7: Scaling Up: Strategies for Sustainable Growth

Becoming isn't about arriving somewhere or achieving a certain aim. I see it instead as a forward motion, a means of evolving, a way to reach continuously towards a better self. The journey never end ~Michelle Obama

As a business gains traction and begins to experience success, the next logical step is to scale up operations. Scaling up involves expanding the size, reach, and impact of your business while maintaining a sustainable growth trajectory. It is an exciting phase that brings with it numerous opportunities and challenges. In this chapter, we will explore various strategies that can help you navigate the scaling process successfully and achieve sustainable growth.

Understanding Sustainable Growth

Before diving into specific strategies, it is important to define what we mean by sustainable growth. Sustainable growth is a long-term approach that focuses on expanding a business while ensuring its profitability, efficiency, and ability to withstand market fluctuations. It involves balancing the pace of growth with the capacity to support it, avoiding overextension that could compromise the overall health of the business.

Establish a Strong Foundation

Scaling up begins with a solid foundation. Before embarking on rapid expansion, ensure that your business's core elements are robust and well-established. This includes having a clear mission and vision, a strong value proposition, efficient operational processes, and a solid customer base. Strengthen your organizational structure and build a cohesive team that is aligned with your business objectives. Taking the time to fortify these foundational elements will provide a stable base for sustainable growth.

Embrace Innovation and Technology

Innovation and technology play a crucial role in scaling up a business. Explore ways to leverage technology to streamline operations, enhance efficiency, and improve customer experience. Embrace automation and invest in tools and systems that can automate repetitive tasks, freeing up resources for more strategic activities. Additionally, foster a culture of innovation within your organization. Encourage employees to think creatively, experiment with new ideas, and continuously improve processes.

Expand Your Market Reach

To achieve sustainable growth, you need to expand your market reach. Conduct thorough market research to identify new customer segments, untapped markets, or even international opportunities. Develop targeted marketing strategies to reach these new audiences and adapt your products or services to suit their specific needs. Consider strategic partnerships or alliances that can help you access new markets or distribution channels. Expanding your market reach diversifies your revenue streams and reduces reliance on a single customer segment.

Invest in Scalable Systems and Processes

As your business grows, it is crucial to invest in scalable systems and processes that can handle increased demands. Assess your current infrastructure, including technology, logistics, and supply chain, and identify areas that may need upgrading or restructuring to support growth. Implement scalable solutions that can accommodate higher volumes without sacrificing quality or efficiency. By proactively investing in scalable systems, you can avoid bottlenecks and operational challenges as your business expands.

Build Strategic Partnerships

Strategic partnerships can be instrumental in scaling up your business. Look for opportunities to collaborate with complementary businesses that share a similar target audience or offer complementary products or services. Strategic partnerships can help you expand your customer base, access new markets, reduce costs through shared resources, or enhance your brand's visibility. However, choose partners carefully and ensure that the partnership aligns with your long-term growth objectives.

Focus on Customer Retention

While expanding your customer base is important, retaining existing customers is equally crucial for sustainable growth. Loyal customers not only provide a steady revenue stream but also act as brand advocates, attracting new customers through positive word-of-mouth. Implement customer retention strategies such as personalized experiences, loyalty programs, and proactive customer support. Continuously gather feedback and adapt your products or services based on customer preferences and needs.

Nurture a Scalable Culture

Scaling up successfully requires a culture that embraces growth, adaptability, and continuous improvement. Foster a culture of learning and development, encouraging employees to acquire new skills and stay updated on industry trends. Empower your team to take ownership of their roles and contribute innovative ideas. Create an environment where calculated risks are encouraged, and failure is seen as an opportunity for learning and growth. By nurturing a scalable culture, you lay the groundwork for sustained success.

Conclusion

Scaling up a business is an exhilarating journey that requires careful planning, strategic execution, and a focus on sustainable growth. By establishing a strong foundation, embracing innovation, expanding your market reach, investing in scalable systems, building strategic partnerships, focusing on customer retention, and nurturing a scalable culture, you can navigate the challenges of growth while maintaining long-term success. Remember, sustainable growth is not just about achieving rapid expansion; it is about creating a thriving and resilient business that can withstand the test of time.

Chapter 8: Managing Finances: Budgeting and Cash Flow for Success

The key to long term survival and prosperity has to do with money management techniques incorporated into the technical system ~Ed Seykota

Managing finances is an essential skill for individuals and businesses alike. It involves effective budgeting and understanding cash flow to ensure financial stability and success. We will take a look at the importance of budgeting, how to create a budget, and strategies for managing cash flow effectively. By mastering these concepts, you will gain the tools needed to make informed financial decisions and achieve your financial goals.

Section 1: The Importance of Budgeting

1.1 Understanding Budgeting

Budgeting is the process of creating a plan for your income and expenses. It helps you track your financial activities, allocate resources wisely, and make informed decisions about your spending habits. A budget serves as a roadmap, guiding you towards financial stability and long-term success.

1.2 Benefits of Budgeting

a) Financial Control: A budget gives you control over your finances by providing a clear picture of where your money is coming from and where it is going. It allows you to prioritize your spending, avoid unnecessary expenses, and make conscious choices about how you use your money.

b) Goal Setting: A budget helps you set financial goals and work towards achieving them. Whether it's saving for a down payment on a house, starting a business, or planning for retirement, a budget helps you allocate funds towards your objectives.

c) Debt Management: Budgeting enables you to manage your debt effectively. By allocating a portion of your income towards debt repayment, you can reduce debt and avoid falling into a debt trap.

d) Emergency Preparedness: A budget helps you build an emergency fund, ensuring you have a financial cushion to deal with unexpected expenses or income disruptions.

e) Improved Decision Making: With a budget, you can make informed decisions about your financial priorities. It helps you evaluate the impact of your choices and make adjustments as needed.

Section 2: Creating a Budget

2.1 Assessing Income and Expenses

Start by assessing your income sources, including salaries, bonuses, freelance work, investments, and any other sources of income. Be realistic and conservative when estimating your income. Next, analyze your expenses. Categorize them into fixed expenses (rent/mortgage, utilities, loan payments) and variable expenses (groceries, entertainment, dining out). Consider both essential and discretionary expenses.

2.2 Setting Financial Goals

Identify short-term and long-term financial goals. Short-term goals may include paying off a credit card or saving for a vacation, while long-term goals may include buying a house or retiring comfortably. Assign a timeline and a financial value to each goal.

2.3 Allocating Funds

Allocate your income towards your goals and expenses. Start with essential expenses and debt repayments, then allocate funds towards your goals. Be realistic about what you can achieve and make adjustments as necessary.

2.4 Monitoring and Adjusting

Regularly monitor your budget to track your progress. Compare your actual expenses against your budgeted amounts and make adjustments accordingly. This process allows you to identify areas where you can cut back on spending and make better financial decisions.

Section 3: Managing Cash Flow Effectively

3.1 Understanding Cash Flow

Cash flow refers to the movement of money in and out of your accounts. It is crucial to manage cash flow effectively to ensure a positive balance and avoid cash shortages.

3.2 Cash Flow Strategies

a) Cash Flow Forecasting: Project your future income and expenses to anticipate cash surpluses or shortfalls. This enables you to plan for any potential gaps and take proactive measures to address them.

b) Expense Control: Keep a close eye on your expenses and identify areas where you can reduce costs. Look for ways to trim unnecessary expenses without compromising your quality of life.

c) Accounts Receivable and Payable: Monitor your accounts receivable (money owed to you) and accounts payable (money you owe to others). Strive to collect payments promptly from customers and pay your bills on time to maintain a healthy cash flow.

d) Emergency Fund: Set aside funds for emergencies to safeguard against unexpected expenses or income disruptions. Having an emergency fund provides a financial safety net and reduces the impact of cash flow fluctuations.

Conclusion

Budgeting and managing cash flow are vital components of financial success. By creating a budget, setting goals, and actively managing your cash flow, you gain control over your finances and pave the way for achieving your financial objectives. Remember, regular monitoring, evaluation, and adjustment are key to maintaining a healthy financial position. With these skills, you can navigate your financial journey with confidence and make informed decisions that support your long-term financial well-being.

Chapter 9: Transitioning to CEO - Navigating the Path of Leadership

Let's first take a look at the stories of two renowned people who became wealthy through side hustles before I show how you can become a CEO.

MICHAEL JORDAN

Jordan, 56, is the highest-paid athlete of all time, but not because of his salary from the Chicago Bulls. Jordan earned $1.4 billion before taxes from corporate sponsorships during his professional basketball career. His film debut, "Space Jam," also earned $250 million at the worldwide box office, according to IMDB. He went on to purchase an NBA team, The Charlotte Hornets, in 2010. The Hornets may be the third least-valuable NBA franchise according to Forbes, but the team's valuation at $1.05 billion is still a major part of Jordan's wealth. Jordan has also made a lot of money from Nike's Air Jordan line, which made him a billionaire in 2015, according to CNN Business.

RIHANNA

Billboard reported that Rihanna, 31, made $22 million from her music in 2016, but that number is dwarfed by her earnings from her fashion and beauty ventures. Rihanna is the creative director of Puma, and she partnered with French luxury-goods maker LVMH to launch Fenty Beauty in 2017 and a fashion house of the same name in 2019. Rihanna's beauty line alone is worth $3 billion, she owns 15% of the company, and she has a net worth of $600 million, according to Forbes.

Becoming a Chief Executive Officer (CEO) is a remarkable achievement that represents the pinnacle of leadership within an organization. It is a role that comes with immense responsibilities and challenges, as well as the opportunity to shape the future of a company. Transitioning into the CEO position requires careful planning, self-reflection, and a deep understanding of the organization's goals.

Some of the key considerations and strategies that will assist you to successfully transition to the role of CEO are highlighted below.

Embracing a Growth Mindset

Transitioning to the CEO role demands a mindset shift from being a functional expert to becoming a strategic leader. Embrace a growth mindset that encourages continuous learning and development. Seek opportunities to expand your knowledge and skills, whether through executive education programs, mentorship, or networking with other industry leaders. Recognize that your personal growth directly impacts the growth of the organization you now lead.

Building Strong Relationships

As a CEO, you will be working closely with various stakeholders, including the board of directors, executive team, employees, customers, and investors. Invest time in building strong relationships with each of these groups. Establish trust, communicate transparently, and demonstrate empathy. Understand the unique needs and expectations of each stakeholder and align them with the organization's vision and values. Building a network of support and collaboration is essential for successful leadership.

Defining Your Leadership Style

Every CEO has a unique leadership style. Reflect on your own values, strengths, and leadership philosophy to define your style. Are you a visionary leader who inspires others with a compelling vision? Are you a servant leader who prioritizes the needs of employees and fosters a culture of empowerment? Are you a data-driven leader who relies on evidence and analytics to make informed decisions? Whatever your style may be, ensure it aligns with the organization's culture and goals.

Setting a Clear Vision and Strategy

One of the primary responsibilities of a CEO is to set a clear vision and strategy for the organization. Define the long-term goals and direction, and communicate them effectively to all stakeholders. Collaborate with the executive team to develop a strategic plan that outlines the steps required to achieve the vision. Establish key performance indicators (KPIs) to measure progress and hold yourself and your team accountable for results.

Building and Empowering a High-Performing Team

A CEO's success hinges on the strength of the team they build. Surround yourself with talented individuals who complement your skills and bring diverse perspectives. Empower your team by delegating authority, fostering a culture of innovation, and promoting collaboration. Encourage open communication, listen actively, and provide constructive feedback. Invest in leadership development initiatives to nurture future leaders within the organization.

Leading Through Change

In today's dynamic business landscape, change is inevitable. As a CEO, you must navigate your organization through periods of uncertainty and disruption. Develop a change management strategy that minimizes resistance and promotes employee buy-in. Communicate the rationale behind changes clearly and transparently, addressing concerns and providing support. Lead by example and embrace change yourself to inspire others to do the same.

Emphasizing Ethical Leadership

Ethical leadership is paramount for a CEO. Uphold the highest standards of integrity and promote ethical behavior throughout the organization. Establish a code of conduct that guides decision-making and ensures ethical practices are ingrained in the company's culture. Make principled choices even when faced with difficult situations, and foster a culture where employees feel safe to report any misconduct or wrongdoing.

Conclusion

Transitioning to the CEO role is a significant milestone in your career, but it is also the beginning of a challenging journey. By embracing a growth mindset, building strong relationships, defining your leadership style, setting a clear vision, empowering your team, leading through change, and emphasizing ethical leadership, you can successfully navigate the path of leadership and make a positive impact on your organization's success. Remember that being a CEO is not just about achieving individual success, but also about creating an environment where everyone can thrive.